# Thoughts
## From
# Dirt 2 Dust

Kenneth Wermuth

ISBN-13: 978-1-6522-4896-5

# INTRODUCTION

You will certainly be able to find many grammatical errors in this "book" whereby I can only apologize for not being perfect, but if this is the case, you should not be perfect either, should you.

You will probably notice some repetitions through the writings, but rather than possibly see this as fill, perhaps more see it as different angles to the perception.

The dates applied are only the dates when I wrote it coherently as prepared herein. Of which the context of the thread, of what I touch on, I started writing about in various forums from back in 1999.

You must also keep in mind that I come from a different part of the world than you, and therefore also from another culture, which automatically provides a different insight.

Although it has been a few years since I had read about the human psyche, whereby there may have been changes, there is still the difference in what is, for example, publicly recognized in your country than in mine. For example, psychopath is publicly recognized in my country, but sociopath is not, why the latter is not mentioned.

*Remember, to condemn a person, you must know the person's life.*

# CONTENTS


Acknowledgments　I

1　Brain Farts　1

2　EGO　7

3　Obligation　13

4　Who Am I　16

5　Defense　18

6　Note　31

7　Undivided　34

8　Divisible　39

9　Identity　46

10　Love　50

11　Lonely　57

12　Live　61

13　Lunacy　68

# ACKNOWLEDGMENTS

Adversity or prosperity, I am after all grateful for it all. Good fortune are few, but gratitude greatest, where adversity is greatest the gratitude difficult, but since I am who I am, the hated is gratefully accepted just as much as the positive gratitude to those who have satisfied life with happy content, which is the most important thing in life. And lastly, for you who are reading this, a big thank you, hope it does not turn out that I have only abused your time.

# 1 **BRAIN FARTS**

(March 9 to 25, 2019)

The inept are only usable when the self is inept...

Is a simple thought just as simple for the simple?

What is neglect for the neglected?

Why is it perfect for the perfectionist not to recognize not to be perfect?

If 1 is alone, is it still alone when there is 2x1...

When the touchy is only themselves why then be touchy over others?

If a psychopath is defined on the basis of errors in the thought paths, why do thoughts not fail about their goal in achieving?

If one pamper is pampered towards another, is it then pampering?

If an assigned fate creates hope, how can a destitute life then have faith in hope?

If justice was law, would law exist?

If the law didn't exist, would you?

If "cleanliness is next to godliness" would you then need water?

Since a need that was missing from childhood, which is demanding for a fulfilled child, is a satisfied there has not been covered and therefore still sought. What is then one's real need as an adult, since this part has never matured? One is only the will of one's parents.

If one is a deceived child, one live through self-deception until one recognizes the child's deception.

Guilt and responsibility are united where responsibility is not borne.

Blame doubled where the subordinated liability is presented.

Pampering without guidance creates childishness.

Greed is a side effect of an unmet need.

Love is a self-imagined illusion.

Acceptance is for oneself, more love than love is through the feeling.

Reflection is a being true images.

Sadness is the effect of the anticipation.

Sincere perception is from a heartless mind.

Original jealousy originates from unwanted recognition.

Envy, on the other hand, is not undesirable, it is a lack.

Lust is one's own lack of presence.

Deceit is a reflection of the core true deception.

Mental illness is emerged from many and therefore not one truth.

One sight is after real conviction.

The hardest truth is always the truth that is closest.

The memory is a liar's worst nightmare.

Revenge is the satisfaction of what cannot be achieved.

Gossip is the fear for self-recognition.

Logic is where all other reason has failed.

Where one is not mistaken, no one else can be right.

Emotional failure arising from self-absorption.

Normal is that, not to differ from what is abnormal.

Normal is one's own conception of other people's recognition.

Abnormal is, without knowledge of what is closest, the truth.

Positive view is the mind's mirror.

Self-deception is the self's defense to live with its conceited reality, which no one possesses.

The responsibility of irresponsibility is passed on to the responsibility of the innocent.

Happiness is to be with joy. Joy is what pleases one. Pleasure is the mind's reaction that response with a familiar emotion, which the mind response back on. So if something does not bring sincere joy, how can the feeling be interpreted as something that gives truly happiness? Is the well-known pleasure of the mind not just another's happiness, or is it truly your own?

Belief is a conviction. A conviction is a definition of one's reality. Pain is the cause of faith, but if the pain is not from a truthful suffering, the conviction will only be after pleasure that pleases one's reality in denial of the true suffering. Can you have faith in that?

If one is in doubt about one's own truth and the truth of one's self is in fear, one can always try to look truly to one's parents and see if the truth pleases one. Is that truthful? or is what we are looking for, only the only thing we want to see the rest of our lives since it is never given in the first place?

If the personality exists in cohesion with the self in pure origin, what can be said to be the essence of its radiance?

If the human spirit has never received openness, can the personality then still be magnanimous?

If the source of life has not been able to flow as intended, towards which direction does the will grow then?

The escaped sensuality is the self-perfection of self.

Wealth dignity seen by most poor.

Malfunction runs in the family, but from where does it starts?

The legacy is passed on from the most important at the most important time in the person's life, through neglect. The fundamental have been laid to secure control of further transfer. What delusion does the "responsible" live after?

1) Everyone else is ill and wrong.
2) How the person lives on -> "forever".

Is it genes or due to the transfer? The child becomes the parent, and becomes just as indifferent to the parent as the parent has been to the child, and because of the lack of self-understanding, transfers the same to own child who again becomes like the grandparents. If it is started with person 1, the child 1 is used by person 1, child 1 then becomes person 2 towards child 2 who in turn becomes person 1, also towards child 1, which gives a total utilization of child 1, from both person 1 as child 2, and so it will continue. The world is built around exploitation. If exploitation is the only thing a person knows about, how can the person see something wrong in being exploited? It is the only form of recognition the person knows about...

Where or how it is started is irrelevant. Most importantly, when does it stop? Are you aware of yourself utilizing one even if you cannot see it yourself? How can we be sure that we know of others only from our own perception, perhaps one's good will is not the best against the one who does not know better...

No matter what you look at in the human psyche, it must be the self-image that creates, both in negative as positive sense.

*"People with a narcissistic personality disorder have a great need to be admired. Freud used the myth of Narcissus, who fell in love with his own reflection to illustrate this need. According to developmental psychology, it is natural to be narcissistic when you are between one and a half and one year old. Everyone knows the little child who has just learned to walk and who is very concerned about others having to notice how good it is. However, it is a stage of development that one would like to get beyond. If you do not, for example. Because one did not get the admiration one needed, one would, according to the theory, continue to have too much need to be admired as an adult. But no matter how much recognition and admiration you get later, it doesn't change that you didn't get enough as a child, and you therefore have an inner sense of emptiness."*

What are you, still an infant?

One of many things I have often thought of and still find strange.

Why does a liar believe another liar then an honest person?

Only thing I can come up with is happy position of common meanness.

# 2 **EGO**

(March 18, 2019)
I am my worst enemy and my name is EGO

I am the one who thrives in every human, I am the brain of the self-centered person and the heart of the narcissist, but I am also the conflict of sincerity and the enemy of love that will constantly conflict with the emotion. I am my worst enemy, even in good times.

Have always liked Freud's view of the mind/personality, and although I think I understand and agree with his models,  there is still something wrong, and since I agree with the idea behind, it can only be the set-up of, for example, the personality model.

Based on the model, the optimum for a human should be a balance between the superego and the Id, that is, equilibrium between these two which brings the personality into balance as a whole, but this seems wrong. Also think that part of this should be seen from the societal norm at all times. Meant, we do not live alone in the world which, as a "better" human, should not revolve around the core of the individual and which should therefore always place emphasis on the super-ego in favor of the Id, since every society with norms (rules and guidelines) will always breed a greater superego and suppress the Id.

But this is only from a slightly black and white view, that there is either only the desire or the norm, for both desire as the norm consists of much more than just the meaning of the word, so at one point the desire can be "turned down" and the norm "turned up" and vice versa at another point, which, under the right circumstances, will equalize and create the balance of the individuals personality. So what I might be looking for is an understanding more specific models that show the different emotional concepts and moral statements that can then be linked and also show the equation of this in a personality.

Always come to this, what are we created of and who are we in reality. It is not so much what we have been through in our lives, it is how we act on this, but again we act on things according to who we are and what we have been through in life. Basically, one person may have been "created" more emotionally than another person, that is, the confluence of the parents' genes. Maybe it is still this, not to see the forest for bare trees? Either not wanting to acknowledge one's own guilt in life or acknowledging a wasted life?

The model does not take into account the development of the child, for this we have to look at other psychologists who really only show the guesses after trying on the child over the different age groups in childhood, each with their own angle of entry who basically all say the same and who still do not give a clear light of the child's mind during development. One thing I know for sure, we are what we learn to be.

I am convinced that who we are born as opposed to who

we learn to be are two different concepts, where the one we have learned we must be, if this conflicts with who we are actually born as, then this will manifest later in life when the developmental process is at its completion or perhaps better said, we go from 0 to 10 and the further towards 10 we reach and the farther from our original self we are, the less opportunity there is for us to ever become who we are born to be. This without that we have self-interest in knowing who we are, but living out from what we have learned, but where there is an "attention" to the self is in conflict with itself, may the possibility of producing something else. Maybe it can be defined as the difference between the mental disorders and personality disorder, even though it is basically the same, but here only to make a difference. The point I try to give is, without opportunities and there where there is hope, because it is common knowledge that the older a person, the harder it is for the personality to change, unless, as stated, it lies to the personality.

I often get away from the point as now (kind of), for the ego it will always be about, but only the individual's feeling is the person's own worst enemy, the cause of much good but also the cause of so much evil.

It can always be difficult but also always the easiest to come up with descriptions observed by or in others, but is it not only the superficial that is the assessment in a description that is only from an observation, because, does it not require much insight into another's life in order to draw a sincerely clear picture of another's personality? It is worse when it comes to the self, but judgments of another/others is and are always based on the judgment of one's self.

In childhood, I was brought up with a very rigid upbringing, which was characterized by many rules and requirements, and often had the idea it was a religious upbringing, but no, although the perception of believe is different from imagination and knowledge. So maybe something to do with myself, probably large parts are from twisted personalities who have only benefited from having power over another creature, not to talk about the hatred that has been associated with this, but somewhere it can also only touch something basic in me, that is, who am I born as? Or is my perception of it, only because my desire is not what is in me?

Because of the same upbringing, I've always had a suppressed Id and an overly ruling superego, full of self-loathing and bad conscience, at even the most ridiculous points, and in some twisted way really always envy the personalities that thrive in desire, though not personalities I would say I love, but mostly because they are the cause of great suffering, not only in my own life but in many. But it must nevertheless be nice not to be bothered but to live in enjoyment. What is best, now that a life in harmony is not intended for all of us?

Too big ruling superego, as mentioned before, as soon as I've been out and the better I've had it the greater guilt always came afterwards, like a bad conscience that came swirling that I had done something wrong, but which has only been due to the fact that I had a good time. Not that I can't feel good, for do what I can to make every day something good for myself, but always connected with being out and where I'm on the way home when the moment of attention is gone , then it strikes me. Got much better with time, but still get affected by it from time to time, and not something I can see a connection with, maybe because it doesn't really touch me anymore? But such a thing is what I mean by ruling superego..

Therefore, it will always (to me) be an interpretation from what I know in my own life if I interpret someone else's life, and with such a superego, very little display of the Id, will be interpreted strictly, even if I myself think that I tend to have an understanding for many behaviors..

One thing that is sure, missing or wrong guidelines in childhood develops Id personalities. This is from infancy where the child does not start to learn the difference between what is acceptable/unacceptable, but what is right for one is probably wrong for another. Now it is also more about norms, where the peculiar thing is that a child may have had a very pleasurable upbringing, but nevertheless in societal "events" can express being well-behaved, so there is an understanding of norms and mostly also a suppression of the Id, but "behind closed doors" is all that is "done" to "feed" the desire. I find that strange, perhaps it is just the difference between being sincere and selfish, that the self-centered always, no matter what, only does things for their own gain, for morality is not in the desire.

Why I really started this with the EGO and worst enemy was with thoughts on what I have touched on defense, this is that where the desire is to dominate, the emotional defense will also be very prominent; nothing will be "done" without it being confirmed by the emotional that pleases the personalities with the defense. Perhaps such a personality expresses its "flaws" and may also show a need for change, that is, a sign that there is morality in the personality, but can that be?

Should it be the case that such a personality with such fierce defenses really wanted change, then it would require a very special personality and would think that it would require a personality brought up with a certain kind of morality, not just something later learned, but brought up .

Such an emotional personality will always relate to the emotion that dominates the personality itself, and when we talk about defense, for the ego, it would always be these feelings that are the person's worst enemy, to have to deal with it and realize who you really are, is ugly, so ugly that the emotions associated with the deception will be so frightening that the personality throughout life will have developed so many defenses to compass for these emotions, the survival of the self.

It is here, even though I can put myself into it, it's weird how people are screwed together. Feeling is what is closest to us, and yet what we see as the most frightening, what we could even end up taking our lives for, rather than realizing that it is our own feelings.

Here it comes in, all this with that we are what we have learned and this with how we are conscious. Because of my childhood, this with the transmitted hatred from an caregiver. I walked around much of my past life and had a perception of what there was in me, was love, where in reality it was the opposite. I reacted to the outside world with a sense that touched my desire as if it was something good, not knowing that the only thing it touched was what I was familiar with, and it was not good, so even though it might have been perceived as a warning, but the perception, perceived the learned, as all it knew.

Perhaps one can look at this "warning" in the same way as when a person is unconscious of a particular emotion which is then confused with another emotion, some express freezing when there is deep fear etc. This is something else and although in my life there is much more to it than what I have superficially described, it is again this with what we learn we should be.

In contrast, the feeling at this point is repugnance and cause the greatest deception man can put on oneself and remain in, in order not to recognize own feelings as they are, strange as we are.

# 3 .OBLIGATION.

(Marts 2, 2019)

We, as a single person, can look into society, and see another person who apparently thrives in a mental/emotional disorder, what rights do we have to interfere with this: that the person's self-deception will only lead to greater suffering which will also aggravate the person's opportunities for improvement? Seems like it's hard as a single person to look at, but what about our humanity? Shouldn't it not be of utmost importance to all of us, are we better than those who have caused this disorder by not relating to the human responsibility we have in a society? But it is difficult to look away from the personal, not only for one's self but also for the person suffering. Are we the ones who feel the best about being passive or is it the denial who wants the best in self-deception? Do we not deceive ourselves; does not one have to live with the suffering of having allowed it to go on? If so, is an intervention in someone else's life not only for ourselves and really not so much for the person we are interfering with?

A child is born and quickly becomes imprinted with

neglect/abuse; the child suffers, and in survival develops a defense against these atrocities which in turn develops another disorder. The child grows and develops more defenses to compensate for the consciousness own awareness around more simple defenses. A defense is the self-deception that we all develop to protect ourselves from the reality we are unable to recognize as being true. We intervene early in life to prevent or reduce the tendency for these types of mental disorders, although defenses may arise and form due to many different circumstances.

The child is grown and come of age, living in a self-deception that strives to please the adult child's emotions and mental imagination, right or wrong is of no importance to the adult child, as defense will always distort the realities, it is survival that weighs most heavily. Without getting into who we were born to be etc. I can only relate to the worse the neglect/abuse, the greater the defense, and therefore also the older the child, the deeper and more extensive the defenses are, to a time when one would think it is incurable.

The child meets the outside world as it is, and often without the outside world forethought that the child is burdened, although there are also the personalities in the outside world who are aware of the child's weakness, thereby only contributing to the child multiple defenses, which really the ignorant are or can be, which will only enhance the child's suffering by confirming the defense and which will also only make it more impossible for the child to get better.  So, in that way, something good can be just as bad as some intentions. Kindness is not always a sign of health.

Again, we see this adult child and we look at this adult child with the disorders in which the personality thrives and where the question lies, what are we entitled in as fellow human beings, what are we committed to?

The worse a defense is or the longer it has existed, the greater the chance of mental breakdown, but at this point we can talk about which psyche, the person's own which is not the personality's own personality, but rather something that has been created, not only to and against others but also to the personality itself. The person lives beside the self and will never fully live their own life. On the other hand, be inactive and the person persists in their own conceited bliss, will live their whole life from a kind of brainwashed state, an applied load that has changed the personality to be different than it originally is, but the personality will suffer no more.

# 4 WHO AM I

## (March 2. 2019)

Who am I? Yes, who are we as individuals are probably the big question of all! Can we say that this is who I am! or states, this is who I think I am? But who has faith in such a life as the earth offers? Why is who I am, who else would want me to be! So it is more appropriate to ask you! Who do you want me to be?

Here, as in private life, I seek what is not possible, peace of mind and heart, what is left of it! My anger is great, but wants suppressed, not provoked! I'm talking from an affected heart! So no evil thought towards the understanding of the feeling! There is only goodness and desire for mutual forgiveness and understanding for life's many injustices...

Many say, live in the moment! But where is their moment when they condemn one of your past? Turn the other cheek, it is said! Only then they can beat one of the other cheeks! Remember who we are today, we are the light of our past! Condemn, and you fail yourself!

Hatred is a big word! And although I have great pleasure to catch those who have condemned my life into hell, and make them feel the pain of the fiery depths of hell! I will still always be trapped in this hell, and their hell must be what they themselves have caused!

Love, yet bigger and stronger words! But who have you really met in life that has had love, more than for themselves? Words are words but by deeds fix is the difference between true hatred and pure love! Understand the love itself, and you begin to recognize others' need for love... Understanding that desire and love are different as night and day! Where in between, must be the border, or what?

Friendships in like-minded unit, is a rare sight, for who would dare? And understandably, since the fear of failure and pain is greater than the desire for peace, but if pain is the road from where we come! So why fear? Is overcome and understanding of self, not the way out of fear? Remember around the now!

Expectations! Interpretation of the others is from the same understanding of oneself! So understand yourself honestly, before you think about other people's expectations, otherwise it will lead to the pain you have expected in life... But yes, do not expect other than what you expect others to expect of yourself!

# 5 DEFENSE

(March 3, 2019)

Many do not know about it, think it may have to do with the army, as defense is mostly not something one think about. Thoughts may only be about how peculiar person is, or in that direction.

It is always easy to perceive defense mechanisms in others, or think that others have a defense, for one-self cannot or it will be very difficult, as it is precisely a defense that is there to protect the core, and can also help others to be perceived as persons with defense.

There are so many different types of defense so this would end up with a lexicon if I were to try to start going into everything, but there are the most prevalent ones.

As with mental disorders, there are disorders that are most prevalent in female as others are in men, at this point it is "abnormal" only where the female is seen in the man or the male in the female. For example, borderline is a widespread disorder in the woman today, but I do look at it in such a way, that because it is already for the woman due to the physiological it seemed more "normal" for a woman to get this term where the problem is greater there where a man is assigned this disorder. Touched because I only intend to touch the woman here.

A small side note. It seems strange that the woman in our society is kind of deprived of the responsibility of taking on a responsibility, something I have always found strange that a woman with great responsibility should not be held accountable. This has meant that next to everyone will seize every opportunity to hold their hand over the woman, perhaps to become more well-liked between women?! Or is it only the mindless who think so? I stand still baffled by this...

I understand all of this around the emotional, how women are easily emotionally affected, but should we as a single person not be able to deal with reality instead of being the reason that the personality should be allowed to live in wonderland?

Has very often had to put up with the accusation of being a male chauvinist because of that, that I am not one who sees difference between people that way, so must of course, also take the responsibility and remain a male chauvinist. It has also always been found that these personalities who very quickly accuse someone like me of being a male chauvinist in reality are themselves feminist, denying..

Now, I would not say that there is anything wrong with being emotional, it is more how this turns out in the personality, even if others have an impact on this, but that's how it is in most things, and also defense.. For a defense is triggered by a personality which in turn can be said to have triggered their defense because of the other's defense, if the first trigger has not also been triggered by the defense, the interaction, the cause and the effect.

A defense is actually triggered due to two things that are really just one thing, the feeling and the perception of. As mentioned before, our perception is formed because of our emotions, which in turn is formed because of our perception, because we perceive something that is connected with the learned emotions which turns out to be a reaction. Can we feel something without being perceived in such a way that it affect us? Wouldn't it always be the perception of something that gives the feeling? Surely a feeling that is perceived can be the cause of another feeling based on the first perception, rather than that which is not felt but is perceived first and is the cause of the feeling. A feeling can be the cause of a memory that is interpreted as good or bad and which in turn will turn out to be a reaction, all in all, the perception is crucial.

It is said that couple therapy should not be practiced in relationships and for the simple reason that where the feeling is stronger the perception will also be the reason for the negative reinforcement. Meant, under normal circumstances, the feelings in a couple relationships are good and great feelings towards the other part, and since we also talk about feelings that can actually not get closer to the self than the love feeling, self-satisfaction, these feelings will also have and get double effect when triggered. Love is shown to be the opposite of the same effect...

There are two kinds of love feelings (based on couple relationships), the most widespread where the feeling is self-centered, where one part actually acts only on own self-perception that even if it is the other part that is the cause of these feelings, then perceive it only on the basis of the complacent, and the second (rather than the first part) where the part has a greater interest in the second (first) part than the self (oneself), although the self-satisfaction is still there, however different as, for example, interest in the second (first) part, perhaps better said, selfish and "altruism", but is difficult to define because we as humans basically always want to be selfish, because even if we say caring, it is due to satisfaction in oneself which has formed the basis for this, that is, for selfish reasons.

The point is, in a relationship where two people are or should be closely linked, defense will also be a frequent cause of conflicts, it is inevitable, unless there is a great deal of connection, indifference or self-acknowledgment between both parties, which we all would probably say is almost impossible, besides very great personal work which requires a great deal of common interest from both parties, which it very rarely does. Many will say, "We are connected" but this is only seen when it is too late. Importance should not be built on imagination.

Signs of whether there is a defense present in a personality can be seen, for example, by whether a person is approachable, because the more close-minded a person is, the greater and more defense there must also be, as is also the case with the emotional, the perception/self-perception.. And in that, as mentioned, that it affects the perception, it affects perception in a lot of areas, because when the most important perception is affected, almost every other perception is also affected, it is the basis of understanding, but one should not mistake one person with defense, for survival can "enhance" the most peculiar reactions, so where you might judge a person as less gifted, the defense, the survival may also turn out to be the exact opposite, although we cannot really talk about gifting or missing talent...

For the most part when talking about defense there is also talk about something on the subconscious level, but personally I am not in favor of this view, as it is more about displacement, denial, self-deception or maybe just forgetting, because can we say to have something unconscious in us? Maybe more around the unknown? But a defense is exactly nothing unknown to the personality itself, for would it be a defense if the self was not aware of it and therefore could not have a reaction from it?!

Early in my life when I did not really know the concept of defense, but also only saw things like what one was conscious of and the unconscious, I quickly found out that all that a person denied and which I therefore assumed was not something the person was aware of, in fact, was something that the person was very conscious of, but really only something that the person would not recognize openly, in this case like hatred as some women at the core will be turn on by. I saw that as soon as it was alone, face to face, it turned out to be something I should perceive as something unconscious, but as soon as there was a possibility that this could be "discovered", the person showed nothing, which can only be evidence that the person was totally aware of the actions and in this case I cannot really talk about displacement, although it may well be one. The point is, I cannot relate to a person possessing a defense that they are not aware of, more to the point that it is about personal character, a personality disorder (unstable emotional personality type).

The understanding that is distorted to adapt one's perception to protect one's self is often exploited by two types of personalities who see only the opportunity to exploit different situations in this world to achieve greater self-satisfaction, such as denial, or exploiting the emotional understanding of others can be difficult to see, since we basically all have an understanding of inner pain, whether this is neglect which is probably the most widespread, but it may be the reason that our empathy for example on this area is often utilized, unless otherwise it is often the reason for utilization.

But these two personality types are the dysfunctional (psychopath) and the insane, and should perhaps write (schizophrenic) but would be inappropriate and is it actually within the psychopathic as well, although here I take more point in the self-centered, where the insane also must be said to belong. However, there is the significant difference that the insane is aware of where I would say that the dysfunctional does not really know about other possibilities. Hard to define, because what drives them is also what can define them as either insane/psychopath or "normal".

Unfortunately, we live in a world that is based on the propulsion of personalities that promote the course of society, that is, keep the wheel going, no matter the expense. For example, it is known that borderline types are types known to produce great "masterpieces" in this world, so based on this, it is in the great interest of "many" to create such personality types, and perhaps not in society interest, but then in their own, here think of knowledge, money and titles, the rapacity which is a great wolf in this world, only the self is at the center, the feeling of satisfaction. For a better understanding of these "masterpieces", for example, look at music and love, which tones are not produced due to the loss of love? What is better, than anyone else suffering than oneself..

Otherwise, the definition of the dysfunctional (psychopath) is based on the cognitive, that is, our thought patterns, the way the brain functions, the "thought" paths that are formed from childhood, the way a person thinks and therefore as a whole perceives things and that which is the center of the psychopath it is self-centered. On a scale of 1 to 10 but all 10 as pure psychopaths, our choices can quickly portray or put us in a learned state as a psychopath.

The insanity cannot really be defined in any other way, for what makes an insane, insane? Most people only know the term from everyday life as that it was insane or psychopathic, but there is a big difference between what we each interpret as sick and what is defines as sick. But really, insanity is a definition based on understanding..

A psychopath does not have an understanding based on anything but the self, so that a psychopath have a great understanding of the world and in a sense also of people, because how else would they be able to thrive in society if they did not understand how they were exploited? I would also say the same about the insane, even though the understanding that makes insane is a delusion of reality, but besides being in the context of a direct well-known disorder, the insane is nevertheless conscious of its condition, enough to conceal it, in the same way as the psychopath.

I started by stating that there are concepts that belong more to the woman than the man and vice versa. Maybe we should look at it more like that from what I have otherwise mentioned. It is more for the man to possess psychopathic traits and insanity for the woman, but again if it is for each to possess these traits, it is only abnormal if the opposite belongs to the opposite sex, and can therefore be described as either a psychopathic woman or an insane man. So a man without self-understanding must be an insane man even though a psychopath has the understanding of himself, more or less, but if the emotional which is more natural in the woman than in the man, then it must be a borderline man who can be defined as insane, which also provides better understanding.

But what about the woman? Can we say a woman without morals/norms is a psychopathic woman? It requires that such a woman be aware of her own self, that is to say, have an understanding of her mind and therefore also some connection with her own feelings, which puts it in a different light, because how can you define an abnormal woman from all this from what defines as normal? For shouldn't it be as with the man that if it is not the woman's possession of these qualities that we can define the personality as being insane? So is the word I'm looking for just that, abnormal? Not fair to the man, but an excellent term for what is not like everything else, abnormal, which I myself am, so is it a judgment on anything other than what is normal?

...rather be hated by the right than loved by the wrong..

The woman, a personality who prefers the self as above everything, but in closer contact I seem to have the perception of a personality that will not be recognized for its own personality, but rather create a confused look at the personality, meant that much is being done to draw attention to the origin of the personality itself in such a way that it is better to know nothing but to know for sure. A little like that it is better to go in an imagination than in knowledge...

Don't know if all this was created to give the woman a supportive self-perception of "being something"? We are who we are, no matter what we can, know or cannot and know! In order to explain this, I must probably elaborate on what I really mean...

If, in order to create a basic understanding, we consider that the woman herself really knows that she has a malfunction (insanity as mentioned), which will therefore only be based on a male worldview, why it may only be this type of man who is a direct contrast to the woman who has put this thought into the world. But nevertheless, the evolution of time has created the basis for having to support what is considered the weak or perhaps this with many men today actually thinking only of the woman either as an object of their own needs, but through this will (as mentioned earlier) do much to win the woman's favor.

Maybe only the woman herself, who created this picture, is

mother to boy's children and is mother not the best in the world? I myself can see what looks like that some people are looking for and find someone who can be their mother, that is, care for them, because they never really learned to fend for themselves. Will always be something there is the reason we are missing therefore is what we seek. Especially if ethics and morals is not in focus through the upbringing!

Perhaps it is only the social development that has created this production, since what I myself think is that what creates society, namely the media, but still with the back thoughts in the upbringing, again an interaction between many things, but only from the development and with the view that we should all be equal, such as has it always been the man who has been at the helm? Why it seems to suggest that something is needed to promote the woman in her way, I do not know, goes blind at this point, because it is unheard of to talk about.

Today through the media there is not the thing that the woman does not possess of characteristics even if for natural reasons it is not really something that lies to the woman, which is why by "examination" it will very often come to "distortions" to get away from the reality of the woman's true nature, which I find deeply strange. Not that I cannot get into the emotional perception, but also have to look at things based on who I am, where I do not see the point in portraying myself as anything but who I am, so why should I say that I am something or can something that I cannot, will it not always turn out to be different when reality knocks on the door?

And it's not because I cannot see it at this point when it comes to achieving, that is, for the people who only present themselves in a special way with that in mind, only to achieve, but it is for me something that belongs to the psychopath and not something I personally want to deal with, but unfortunately the world is a good place for such personalities.

I touch thoughts from the point of view of society or the view of the most widespread man, from the "things" that the world gives of information and clearly also from my own experience. I do not look at the woman and see an insane personality, in certain type of women I do, the same way I see the psychopath in certain types of male personalities. What just like "interest" me more is in the areas where otherwise "normal" personalities follow the crowd without knowing what they are actually following and doing about themselves, but only follow because it is widespread or because everyone else does, maybe only to get accepted? Others are more important than their own well-being! Strangely, choose life but follow death.

As mentioned, insanity is not seeing reality as it is. So, not oneself to inflicted judgment, to give oneself, to exhibit oneself as anything other than who one really is, not exactly what is the beginning of what one cannot or will not understand reality as it really is?

…what you see is only what you are willing to realize…

Maybe this will be the last addition, I am not one who sets about writing something from a plan and therefore do not make mind mapping, even though I have an idea of something I want to touch on, which is just as often the only thing that is not touch, is quickly led by the path of thought.

Other people's perception of my person has always been of no importance to me, however, not from the person(s) I love, and not that it has changed my person in that way, but do we all not have it like so, that acceptance deep down is something we all seek in some sense? It probably has more to do with what we are willing to "do" to achieve this acceptance or from what "form" this seeking of acceptance is formed, thus "form" as what is the reason for this and this acceptance seeking being formed. That is, it is probably all about acceptance originating from childhood, we can probably discuss whether an acceptance seeking first appears later in life and therefore it is due to some experience through life that has been the cause of this acceptance seeking, but there must still be some basis in childhood, perhaps the search itself, perhaps the self-understanding of being accepted in all points and all from childhood can come to this later, just as the child is more mature and finds out the reality, which is somewhat contrary to the fact that it was created in childhood.

Just want to say that if one seeks an acceptance from another that has never been obtained, then it will probably never be given, so why seek what is doomed to be unattainable? Conscious or not, such will never be easier said than done. But nevertheless, it will always have power over the seeker, but no need to be accepted by some who cannot even accept themselves...

For myself, I would say. Think more it has developed into something else, a kind of hope.. If people accept me that is ok, they do not, well it is also ok, we are all different and why should it get to me if those who are different than who I am, do not accept me? It is more important that the person(s) I find "commonality" in, accept me otherwise there is something wrong.. Are we not a group, we are not all or nothing? Can we allow ourselves to say I like that and that, but that and that I do not like,  so I take what I like and let the rest die, is that not, exploitation? Because yes, if you only accept half, then you have to utilize the leftovers in such a way that you still see a person as a whole personality, shouldn't you?

Personally, I know that the only one I have ever really needed to be recognized by is the partner that I was fortunate/unlucky to be allowed to become acquainted with in life, and in my life it is now my whole life (monogamous) that is, of body and soul. However, it is not a matter of course that there should be recognition of one's person in a relationship, perhaps not for everyone, but for me it is of crucial importance that appears in the attention one has for one's partner, maybe twisted, but simplicity is not my strong side.

Finally, when and if one reads someone else's thoughts and if one have an interest in understanding what one choose to read, then what one reads can also have a negative effect on oneself, but only self-evident. As with people in the real life with defense, such personalities are often unwilling to realize that the feelings that arise in them are their own feelings, perhaps it is conscious emotions that others bring forth in them, but very often it is the reaction to one's own emotions and since it is a defense that one cannot bear to contain, this aroused emotion is always transferred to the person who evokes the emotion, and since it is perceived in the self as a very unpleasant feeling, the other person is also a very unpleasant person, which can result in other defenses.

Example, from what I myself have experienced in life from time to time this type of transfer which is really called "projective identification", that is, one person is assigned and assumes another person's identity/behavior, it "is sent/arises" mostly from an emotional personality if we can talk about borderline.

Of necessity, and in a good mood, I turned to a female personality, where I afterwards wondered about the "emotional change", my mood gone from good to almost hostile. And when I look back on the situation it seems more like I have been a spoiled mom-boy who did not get his will. The point is, it transferred, not something that came from me but probably more because of the person's frustration (still keep in mind, the interaction). In contact with the same person, I did not think about it the first time, the second time I became aware of it and hopefully if there is a third time, I will be fully aware of what is really going on or the way it can be done. Maybe it can only happen in the circumstances, where one do not expect it and therefore one are not aware of it.

Has been a third time since, but this time it was only a good contact, but nothing was causing frustration either.

# 6 NOTE

(February 28, 2017)

## Note on Notes...

Yet another peculiar note from a peculiar person describing the peculiarity of the peculiar.

Have for a number of years been involved in many debates with many different personalities, only to find that the vast majority do not debate with that in mind as one should think a debate is for, but in fact only debate for self-assertion reasons.

However, this is not always the case, although one can quickly be cheated, because out of everyone I have tried debate with, I would say that maybe 1 in 10 is one who is debating for the sake of the debate, but one can be cheated quickly. of those personalities who are more self-centered than those who only seek to emphasize themselves, namely the cunning ones. Those who more consciously "fish" for information and through this "fishing" highlight themselves for being serious in a debate, but who will nevertheless appear as parasites. It is these personalities who are more conscious use knowledge that they basically do not comprehend.

The difference between these types and which is clear in a debate is that the latter types are presented as knowledgeable and arranged in the debate process, with little cautious progress and a huge search for information on what their next step should be. As the first type, they do not want an opportunity for them to appear "ridiculous" from their own view, but they are more indifferent, where the first type is more emotional about this. Still, it always turns out to be a waste of time.

The first type mostly has some kind of delusions of grandeur in their display, they are so oblique to their own view that they do not think very far, and their behavior is evident when others point out their mistakes, but because of their basic uncertainty this type quickly turns out to be bottom kissers, makes many attempts to distort the meaning of the word to another meaning so that it will appear the same as another/others have pointed out, but, for the most part, they always exhibit childishness and the swift end of debate, but can occur many strange reactions from such an unstable personality.

Attention in well-being will automatically create many people with a search for the same, it is inevitable, it is the amount that sets the framework for the individual's development especially when the individual is left to the influence of society.

I started by "debating" or trying to debate the web almost 20 years ago on a number of different forums. Facebook has only aggravated the progress of these personality types as truly dominating as they are so many and since that is what the world is developing. For the most part, the forum is closed and opened reset, where I have been active in debate. On Facebook, I am mostly thrown out, and only because emphasis is violated.. It is a rarity to experience the opposite. Best, in most places, is to keep silent or "play" ignorant to be allowed to follow.

The groups are still infested with aphids that are destroying the origin, but are believed to be in some places that accept the basics. But time has created many threads in which much has been formulated for lack of understanding, which is why I sometimes find a need to express myself in my own company..

Isn't it better to chop your own leftovers down rather than one of the crowds to hack their perception into the stone? "Rest in peace, you are missed" - if you can believe in that.

# 7 **UNDIVIDED**

(February 28, 2017)

Emotions are really something twisted quirks, life and the world would be a better place without it, it is really the cause of everything bad! What would exist of the 7 sins of death if the feeling did not exist? (pride, greed, fornication, jealousy, gluttony, anger and laziness) But is it not just that, where it acts as a negative intention?

Still, feeling may be the cause of the greatest joys this earth can offer, but that's not what drives, if nothing else, not in me personally. Even though I live my life to make every single day a good day, the day will never be able to contribute to the appease that life has brought me, really peculiar. Although I find joy in even the smallest thing, it is only a moment denial of reality..

Emotions are in the self or due to the self; it is an interaction as mentioned before, consciously due to the emotion and feeling due to consciousness. I am due to my feelings which in turn are due to self. I know that the emotion is not in the physical but that the experience of the physical informs my consciousness of how to perceive something so that my emotions are learned, but why can't I disclaim it and still maintain the feeling? Perhaps it is due to the preservation of the only thing I know what is and therefore know about, although it is too easy to relate to it, but it also has an impact, because how can we as individuals seek something we do not know when we only know what we have learned? We can learn hatred from infancy and see this as love for how should we know differently? Can't we learn love without the knowledge of hate? Isn't the opposite also a great opportunity and probability for some people!?

However, I can only take the words from my own life and from others, from the experience I have observed through contact with others, where I see here the many inscrutable paths of life, but are we all doomed to go a certain way through life or is the path only the one you either choose for yourself or the one that others do not want to go? Last one is very likely, second last less, for which man wants to go where no one else wants to go? Can only be two options because it is right or because it fits best with what you have learned/been, where the last mentioned probably requires more ignorance, lack of other opportunities and/or perhaps indifference.

I know of, for example, cutters, not the ones that only scratch themselves, but really the ones that cut deep in themselves. Was 17/18 years ago somewhere over a period where I met a young man, Michael he was called, really quite nice, but with great pain, so large that his scars after coalescing were almost an inch wide, which says a lot about where deep that was cut and the scars were long. We can ask ourselves that question, was it to feel or was it to get away from another pain? Many do not want to see or recognize the pain of others, perhaps because it hurts, maybe because they are too cold? Self-Interest?

Again this with the feeling that is so close to us that it

either denies or goes directly into the blackboard. Can only have something to do with the personality itself, namely the self-awareness needed to realize who one is, which can therefore only be required through experience of pain in life, everything else from childhood must, by later internal pain, take on the path of denial or what? If we are who we learn to be, then how can we learn it later in life and here I do not think in the direction of, such as going to school and learning how to study, probably a person can learn a subject and also through this learning achieves or has the basic understanding of the subject, but there is a great difference between knowing something and understanding something.

Is it all up to the individual, namely the choice, to abandon the past to face a new future that you are unfamiliar with? Although I do not think that it is a simple choice, because how do you discard yourself without becoming someone else and maybe someone else you do not want to be, then it is not always that simple. Can we pick out a single emotion or memory associated with an emotion and at the same time remain ourselves?

The recognition of who we are must be firmly rooted in the self in order for cognition to remain an acknowledgment or else we are no better than what causes negative emotions in this world and it is only through this process that a new step can be taken, there can be no other possibilities. While this does not remove a person's current situation about what, why and how, it is like stomping in what you are put into or in this world for..

The immediate feeling is reinforced by our focus on it, so of course it is a natural reaction to ignore such feeling, that is, as long as it touches negatively, which makes me think of personalities that are always said to see the positive in things.. Heard about them, but never met one, although I have met many who say they are positive even though it has always turned out to be the opposite.. Seems unlikely, but everything is possible, so why not?!

Since feeling is the nearest and closest to an individual, it is difficult for me personally to be able to deny what is going on in me, but since feeling is a direct cause of the development of defense, it can be difficult to say if my opinion is or can be an imagination, because it is the effect of the defense, to protect the personality from unwanted "experiences", but now there are many undesirable experiences I would like not to be there, but even if focusing on the recognition of one's self can be a developed one defense, in such a way that one can maintain the "belief" in oneself that one relates properly to things/reality, from the fact that one then does not have to realize that life has nothing to offer, everything is over..

I know I am a strange one and can probably give an explanation of each behavior pattern I exhibit, but still searching for answers, which I will probably do two the day I get single room with a lid.. Have often searched my life and just so often wondered why I am who I am and what may have made me who I am. Last one is really easy enough, but I think the big question is probably more, are we born as anything other than what we have learned we should be? Hard to say when the memories are in the mirror of their own perception.

…only based on what is normal, I'm different…

Surely we all know how to be hurt and sometimes to "punish" ourselves to make ourselves sad? Why is this always only in the context of good memories which is fundamental to, for example, the lack that is in us, which requires that we do not deny everyone who suggests negative sign against ourselves about people. I myself know of shame, a disgusting feeling when it hits, and here I am not thinking about being ashamed of anything at the moment the shame arises, but the shame that comes in flashback over previously experienced events is not nice and I also try very hard two push it astray, displace it, which I don't always think is easy. Oddly enough, this doesn't have to be a real shame, but maybe just something that is made to a shame, not by oneself, but by who has "transmitted" the shame, which in such a situation should not be something one should feel ashamed about anymore, but it remains a shame. Both because the disgust and because it is therefore suppressed, it should not, since the consciousness of its origin is acknowledged, which should therefore make it what it really is, inflicted... Is the feeling of shame worse than the sense of responsibility, and why is it?

From time to time, I still get the feeling of shame from an old time and I am well aware that I should not feel ashamed of these flashbacks, but it has the same effect on me every time, perhaps because they come as unexpectedly as a blow from the abyss that leaves me breathless? And strangely enough, I have memories of events in my life that I should probably feel ashamed of, but see it either as fun or that's just the way it was and there's nothing to do about it. Strange what constitutes a personality...

So all in all, we have learned an emotion or better, we have learned to act on an emotion which in turn must be based on who we are in fact born to be, the senses, the genetic which really still does not say anything...

# 8 DIVISIBLE

(February 26, 2017)

Emotions are really something peculiar. Every human being is conscious of its senses and yet not everyone is self-conscious, which in itself is a contradiction, for we are all conscious of our senses, like every creature on this globe, for there is no great difference between animals and people other than the fact that we humans emphasize ourselves to be much more than what an animal is, for even animals have thoughts, they can plan and therefore also speculate, so based on this, the only difference can only be our perception of what is right and wrong, which basically only stems from having to be civilized, have a moral view based on what is right and wrong. But no, even though it sounds good for "them"...

A new born child which is born completely senseless will remain unconscious, both of the self which is the outside world, there is nothing to stimulate anything, even if the child is born with a pulse, it is not possible for such a creation to ever develop, it will be as short as it lives and remain a blank board.

I used the word "its" in the beginning: "man is conscious of his senses" as the senses are crucial to human consciousness, for if the hearing is inhibited from birth this will also affect parts of consciousness, yet other parts of the consciousness will be elevated which a "normal" hearer will not be aware of. This is the case in all areas, including the more genetic intertwining of our ancestry that constitutes us as individuals, not to say that we are an equal division between our parents, for one may resemble one parent but may have the cognitive structure following the other parent. No matter what, I want to relate as a whole, even though we are made up of our parents, that we are created as a unique individual who basically makes us who we are/become.

As infant, thinking about what we are as basic, that is, both our appearance and our thought patterns. Appearance gives us a perception of the world in a certain way, how do others act on how we look and what will this create in us!? Our patterns of thought/cognitive "tell" ourselves how to perceive what we perceive and which, later in life; appear in the way we present ourselves to the outside world. It is all an interaction between everything and nothing. We are born, influenced and live by the only thing we know about.

I also started with the emotions and moved on to consciousness, but it is strange how we develop so differently from one another. Clearly our senses are mixed together from the moment of creation which then also makes a difference in our emotions, although it may not be crucial as long as we are not talking about any defect which can be described as abnormal from what belongs to that witch go under the description of being an Homo Sapiens. Meant that even if a personality like an infant has an emotional feeling perception than another personality, the infant still feels, which also from what I have mentioned will affect the self-consciousness, I doubt that in such a case not only will sharpen the perception on other points as I also mentioned.

Think that what I am trying to find words for myself is that the difference starts and lies in the stimulus we are surrounded by from infancy, which lies away from the topic "ourselves". The fact that we can actually say that we are all met equally, but is made unequal, because even though we consist of genes that are different from each other and which should also form the basis of who we are/become, but should this make a crucial difference , now that it is also intended that the one we consist of are also the ones that stimulate us, which should fit as a key in a lock, where it is that others who are not of the child's genes will have difficulty in "opening" the child's "lock" and therefore only "put" the child in a "closed" development process.

Funny, all this started only with the fact that I was thinking about partnership again, which I have from time to time thought about a lot through life, what do we look for, what do we meet, what personality do we find interesting, what is the reason we looking for a partner, what difference is there between the self and the self that we meet/seek... Which then comes to these thoughts as it always does.

Have actually always thought about such a thing as with "beauty", what is it in me that makes me have the view I have for example on "things" that I find pleasing in some appearance. I do not think that I have been given an upbringing that has emphasized that something must look certain that something is of greater worth than anything else. Although part of such a perception may come and develop later in life, what we are imprinted with and which we come to understand as something of worth, but there is far from thinking of a color, a form, a taste to thinking of another human being, even though the difference is probably not so far apart?

After I got divorced, I only thought about this even more, with a greater focus on the search for a partner. Do not know if it is natural that our own private thoughts go first on our "wishes" that "I WILL HAVE". Know that I cannot relate to such a thought, because one is what I want, another is what can be done in relation to everything else I "want". For in that I personally see a partnership as most valuable in life, it cannot be of much value if it is only according to what one "want", it is therefore an impossible thought.

For something to be valuable in this view I have, it has to be something harmonious, something dynamic, but is it again not just saying what you want? Some find that there is only agreement in a partnership, others find that there should not be much in common, and the vast majority only meet one another and it evolves as it once does, clearly based on who they each are, that is, childhood, upbringing and inheritance...

Genesis expresses the difference between woman and man as follows: (AKJV)

[21] And the LORD God caused a deep sleep to fall upon Adam, and he slept: and he took one of his ribs, and closed up the flesh instead thereof; [22] and the rib, which the LORD God had taken from man, made he a woman, and brought her unto the man. [23] And Adam said, This *is* now bone of my bones, and flesh of my flesh: she shall be called Woman, because she was taken out of Man. [24] Therefore shall a man leave his father and his mother, and shall cleave unto his wife: and they shall be one flesh.

Which gives a very good insight that we are looking for what we lack, that is the man lacks what the woman has and the woman lacks what the man has.

Personally, from a simple point of view which is only adapted to this example, I've always looked at it like this "I lack the heart that my chest will cherish, but since the wrong woman will be more the missing bone, this woman will also be ruthless against the emptiness trying to protect her. Only the right woman will fill a man from the emptiness she consists of."

It just doesn't help that much, because what is one's "longing" or what is missing from this "longing", the interaction...

Do think what I lack in this equation, is the world we live in, for does this world offer this lack? In certain cultures and as it once was in our culture, it was that/them who cherished us and who knew us best, and who therefore only wished us the best in life, our parents, those who "approved" a partnership. Where in our world today, in the cultures where it still goes on like that, probably it is more about money/items/titles that are the most important, that is to say, not what is most important to us, but to them, the parents? But I wonder if in many such cases, it has also become the "child's" interest which is the parent's interest, for the child can only be of different perception if the child is self-conscious..

In that we walk on our own legs and in that we move in a notion of who we are and therefore also who others and the world are, it is that we meet with others who in most cases are probably only doomed to division. Some remain enough in the notion of who they are and who their partner is, and what is intended for them, but see the world today, where the highest is only the desire and therefore also appearance, not to talk about money and titles.. Can we say that 9 out of 10 end up going from one another?

Sure, the desire can be hard to disregard, but personally, a quick bang is not of any greater worth than the very worthy one that lies in the mind of what I first look for, then the harmony between the inner and outer is the next. But hard, yes...

Self-awareness is the key word, but will not everyone and everyone say that they are self-conscious!? But can we be sure of that? Doesn't it really not just require one wrong self-perception to say that we were wrong? I know what I know, but can I say with certainty that what I know is not only what I think I know, imagination.. The feeling of what I am willing to realize about myself tells something about my self-awareness, so since it is so, I also can't say that I am self-conscious, as it in itself tells me that I live in a conception about myself, but I can say that all my life and until the day I die, I will go towards being more self-conscious than I was yesterday, because only by knowing that I know, I also know that what I do not know is just something I think I know, and therefore when I know, I will also know what I'm missing..

But again, an impossible thing, because how can one seek self-recognition without a mirror to look in? Then again, it requires the appropriate mirror.. If it is a mirror that cannot reflect, it is only an empty frame on a wall, unless it is the frame missing from one's own image...

What fits, what doesn't fit, what do we resigned ourselves with? Since a partnership for me is something of valuable, and with what I touch, a partner is and the part of me that makes me whole, thus one's best friend, the one you do everything for and who also does everything for one, but not only superficially, for the consciousness of one and the other, shows through how the dynamics are, where even the smallest grain of sand can destroy the harmony and create emotional disturbances between two people. The wavelength.. You give and take, you take and you give...

The perception and understanding of words can also often show what self-awareness a person is in. A little like we learn from childhood when a word is to be interpreted negatively or positively, where the person who is away from self-perception often sees words as something other than just words to express something, although even a person with self-knowledge can see words as negative/positive, but probably more from the situation itself. And funny enough, even the biggest denying personality may well show self-recognition if the wording is given correctly, but on the other hand, even the same personality will only perceive the same wording negatively even if the wording is presented very positively to the personality, only the self-perception and understanding of the meaning of the word, as well as the perception of the other party as dictating how something is interpreted, peculiarly..

# 9 IDENTITY

(February 25, 2017)

Identity, what is it really and can we be sure that our identity is ours?

There are really only two essential forms of identity, firm that is stable and loose that is unstable.

There is really not much to say about the stable, it remains unchanged at the person's choice, although it can be changed, improved or worsened, but either by choice or for example, by trauma.

The unstable has the same characteristics as the stable, can be changed in the same circumstances, although the change here can take many faces as disguise and therefore in most cases will be a stable false identity.

We have many different personalities, each with our own identity that makes us who we are, that is what we are characterized by. Some are designated strange as they deviate too much from what is assumed to be normal, that is, the personalities that make up the majority in a society. Not to say that usually then also is normal, because what is normal if the normal is only based on what is most common?

But we can probably boil down all the different types of personalities to a few.

Those who have an interest in finding recognition in themselves and are presumed to have a fundamentally stable identity, for it can only be part of their identity of knowing who they are and maintaining or create improvement.

Those who also possess a stable identity with who remain who they are until they are hit by trauma or die. Here, the topic is more about personality disorders, and since it is a fixed identity, the likelihood of change/improvement is too small for a change to occur.

Back there is the unstable identity, of which the same situations can be found as under the stable, but the intention is that it requires much more of the person self and/or others to help, in order to achieve a true identity and a lot of work in order to maintain something which can be referred to as stably.

The major problem with unstable identity is the reason that it is unstable and/or remains unstable.

Our personality is formed throughout childhood, where we can say that on the basis of the basic formed personality, the identity is "determined" through and after our maturation process. That is, when are we really mature? Some are very old but still very immature and some are young and very mature, so to say that it is when the teen age is over we cannot. Nor can we assume that it is a ongoing process, even if we are constantly "growing" mentally, or we should. It still comes to the basics, the personality formation in childhood, which just underpins maturation and how the "final" identity develops.

Childhood can have as many nuances witch can or will cause problems later on, and not even having to be badly inflicted on the child, can be an imagination due to something else that lies a bit astray in the unconscious, though I am not an supporters of something unconscious in the way it is usually used. But the cause can also be a direct "evil" that the child has been opposed to, although it can also not be said to be a direct cause, for such a thing can also have the opposite effect on the personality, namely, to early maturation. It is therefore very difficult to say anything directly.

The point of all this is some of the very widespread causes and deterioration of unstable identity, namely the self, self-perception, perception of how others perceive one, etc. all things that affect low self-esteem, again due to many different reasons which again are not needed to originate from something other than self-delusion. Got the understanding that just the first time a woman reaches her period may be enough, the self-esteem is been confirmed through the self-imagination and everything else as mentioned above.

When I started, I had a clear direction in what I wanted to write, but after taking a break I have moved away from the direction a bit. What caused me to start writing was not only that of identity, but some of the defenses that unstable or non-identity creates or mechanisms that the non-identity person had to contend with, such as assuming the identity of others to maintain self-affirmation.

This that their self-esteem is so low that they cannot reasonably have normal contact with others without having a negative impact on themselves and those whom they have contact with.

Is or should the question for everyone not be, who we sincerely are, and not who we have it good with at imagining ourselves to be, because only through understanding and acknowledging our true self can we only acknowledge who others are , so who are others to you or who are you to others?

# 10 **LOVE**

(December 4, 2015)

**(Danish words: kærlighed = love, which in word play consists of two words: honesty in love: ærlighed = honesty)**

Love, the essence of feeling, most people will relate to it, but is it?

We are conscious do to our senses, of which the feeling must be said to be the most important and crucial sense for "healthy" self-awareness, but the feeling does not have a perception of itself, it is controlled by our thinking, consciously or unconsciously, we act on the outside world based on what we perceive as we also act on our emotions which is a reaction to this "sense" of the outside world we perceive, an dynamic effect, or that is, as an individual, a dynamic act must take place before we can talk. about a "sensibly healthy developed "feeling/awareness", because if the interaction between feeling and understanding is out of step with reality, there is imbalance in perception which cannot therefore be described as something dynamic.

Still, it does not clarify what love really is, because we mostly like/love what we are used to or what is learned, because how else should we relate to something we do not really know anything about? Meant, we are born blank and our emotions are "set" according to our upbringing which affect our understanding/perception, so that even though we all know deep inside good and bad, and not only for ourselves, but for everyone in connection with good/love feelings, then we do not know each other's self-perception of the love feeling because we are of different heritage and environment, which precisely touch the individual's "need" for self-satisfaction.

Self-satisfaction sounds very self-centered, but isn't that the biggest focus in this world? And even though we are different and it therefore is not the same for everyone, then it is exactly for everyone, what is ultimately the same for everyone, namely love, either to ourselves or to another who affirms something within a self that meets some kind of love/need feeling. For example, I do not love myself and I am conscious of this, cannot see any "advantage" in having to love myself; it will not change anything in me in a positive direction. Then some will say that if one cannot love oneself, then one cannot love others, which is not quite correct, for not loving oneself, do not touch that one do not know what love is, will even say that one may be more conscious of what love is, why one also know that love must be real, that it is a feeling that cannot be true if one love oneself, because how can one love someone more than one love oneself, as the feeling itself as touching love cannot be replaced by a feeling that is really another.

What I really mean by the above is this with the difference between the dynamic and the disturbed self-perception, because one is not self-conscious about this, at this point, that if one cannot or will not acknowledge that it is the feelings of others that give one a feeling of love, that is, to thrive in one's own feelings rather than in the contact between others, then one has only love for oneself and will probably therefore only "give" that feeling to others as "tricks" it in the other that "gives" the feeling towards a self that thrives in one's self.

The point here is probably that if one cannot disregard oneself, then one cannot love another based on a true love feeling.

But still based on my own reality of love and not because I do not love myself and that no matter who we are, it nevertheless comes to a satisfaction that meets one's needs. I can quickly get feelings for others, feelings like care for/like, need only correct circumstances, even if I don't love myself, but this feeling still gives me some kind of self-satisfaction in liking, even though it is me who has the feeling of care for someone else. I affirm myself in my sense of others through what is probably acceptance of my person. Don't we all do that? Are there any differences in "loving" someone else if we talk about a true feeling? That through our conception of mutual feelings do we love ourselves, either more or if one does not love oneself in advance?

It gives a somewhat different picture than what I mentioned earlier, because this could give a picture that not loving oneself seems more like a reason for seeking to love someone else in order to love oneself or being that only to be able to accept oneself, perhaps only to have a purpose in life? Whatever it may be, on the more subconscious level, for the one who loves himself, yet diverges.

Thoughts always evolve for me in writing, so I deviate from what was really my original point/question, so I don't really remember, but think it was just something like "what is love really", because love is different from person to person, even though, as I said, we all know deep down what is right/good - bad/wrong, only the impulsive gives the difference not knowing the difference. Still, there is a lot in this quote: "Do to others as you want them to do to you".

In our younger days, our thoughts may not so much be on such a thing, whether it is for some or it takes "age" or maturation of emotions to try to understand something like that? So to give a better understanding of what I mean about self-perception of love, I will try to give a description (in negative view) that sets up a point of how something might go wrong on love/emotion as something that is right and something that is wrong, that is, all of it is something we learn which is not always our own feelings.

Although the whole childhood is of great importance for the development, but the foundation on which everything else is built is and always will be crucial, even though the child at all times can suffer, as a life also can at any time in any one age. One's caregiver is once the one we learn from, is characterized by and therefore also the one(s) that is the reason that our feelings/perceptions are or become as they are (in the vast majority of cases). So if we receive hatred where we should have received love, we may not later be aware of this or perhaps be aware that there has been something wrong or still is, but unable to/would realize what effect this has had on us and still has. The point is, love is replaced by hatred which therefore something that will persecute us without us really being aware of it. It is replaced because it is what we have learned, it is not something we choose or want to realize as something that is wrong, since it has come from the person(s) we should have received care from (our mirror), so as it affects self-esteem and therefore, something very basic in our identity is something that, for "natural" reasons, will develop defenses in our personality, making it difficult to realize. If we relate and to the difference between the basic development and the subsequent, it is as if, basically, the bias automatically removes the personality from its sincerity and opens the back door for direct defense, where it subsequently holds the personality against its sincerity and subsequently defends onto. The difference is, easier and difficult opportunity for correction.

Throughout life, maybe you meet partners in small relationships that do not allow further development, although any such contact will also affect one's further development and which only helps to mature our emotions, so we are "ready" for the day when it begins to become more serious, and really something we have learned, not only through our parents, but also through social norms.

As described earlier, from a more black and white view, there are two kinds of personalities in this area, the difficult and the easier, which we therefore consider that the difficult is more absent from the self, and the easier perhaps have a better awareness of the sincerity of the self. Because does it not require the right circumstances before an attention is brought to life? When or who is needed before something comes to the surface, where the personality from childhood has been characterized by experiences that are against the self's sincerity? Does it not require the same key as initially opened the insincerity?

If attention from the caregiver has been negative towards the child and therefore the child has inadvertently sought recognition from the this person, it will have a great impact on the self, depending on the need and the size of the negative, but at some point this will shift attention from what is needed to what is given, after which that witch is given is what is normal and what is needed, is abnormal. The caregiver will always be imprinted in the child's self that is avoidable. And since a child always needs recognition from a caregiver, that is, recognition through love, then love in connection with such a mind as the caregiver possesses will also always be perceived as what it knows. Could it be different?

Life is lived normally and where the importance to the person has lived only with the perception that person once has. Life has not yet provided opportunities that put the personality into a situation that gave rise to further attention to the self itself. Until the day when the child meets a personality reminiscent of the caregiver. How will this turn out? Isn't this predetermined? If you are aware of life, have you not yourself noticed how many actually end up with a partner who is reminiscent of either their father or mother? Ask yourself why...

So from this description, what one thinks is not always what it is. It can be incredibly difficult to find out, and doesn't really mean that you can later find out what your own love is, maybe it's easy for those who have never been challenged in childhood, maybe they're just some who has never come to realize otherwise? There is usually a reason why you start to realize something, because if there is no doubt, there is no cause.

It has been many years since I became aware of this, and yet will not say that I have become particularly wiser about what true love is. That is, in me love is associated with sincerity, but it is my love or the one that I give and which I therefore also want to give, which again comes to this, the acceptance of one's own feelings, although in this case it is one's own feeling that another has the same feeling towards one as one has towards another, which in turn is a self-affirmation of one's self. But can it be said to be love or is it not just a small part of love?

Maybe you cannot realize love if you have never received or experienced love, but no matter what, love is a union in something mutual, which must be the acceptance of the self as also the other's self, on a level that is either the same or a plane on agreement!? Maybe love is just that one's needs are met, nothing more.

*"It must be heavy. To wear that facade all the time. Breaking same tears. When the forces runs out. And you're forced to look in the mirror. But do not know yourself. Naked. Dissolved. Staggering. Broken. That's not what you dreamed of, was it?" (unknown origin)*

# 11 LONELY

(December 3, 2015)

## Are you lonely?

On Facebook I have been a member of various "Single/Lonely" groups, which just made me think a little about this, not because I haven't given it a thought before, but I don't always get affected by the same thoughts or feelings that give specific thoughts.

The question I really wanted to ask in the group, than until I realized that the active people in it probably more looked at it as a dating group for single people, which in that sense has nothing to do with loneliness, but more something to do with be desperate for some meat.

The question was: Are any of you really thinking about why you are or have the feeling of loneliness? For one can be lonely and one can feel lonely, which is not the same, although being lonely also gives the feeling of loneliness, where if one only feels lonely it does not mean that one is lonely.

One may well be lonely for many reasons, not be accepted

as one is, which may have its causes, both self-stated, but also for more "bleak" reasons, where bleak may as well be of clarity to the bleak.

It may be that you are just impossible and cannot or will not be organized, whereby most people turn away from the person. It can be something with social anxiety, which probably touches the feeling of loneliness, though loneliness is very real. My point is, are we all not really lonely where the difference lies in wanting to recognize the loneliness or feeling of loneliness?

If we all really feel lonely, whether we want to acknowledge it or not, it is precisely because we are seeking an acquaintance that is like ourselves, something we can identify ourselves with, something we can feel confident about? Maybe for some/many?

Personally, I very much doubt that this is what is moving in myself, because in many ways it might seem like a pleasant thought, that there was someone with whom you agreed with and has the same interesting as yourself, but don't even think I could endure being with such a person. So probably, the more contradictory, the most development I see?

I know there is a big difference between being lonely and having the feeling of loneliness, of which the feeling will probably seem so dangerous to some that it is not a feeling that will be looked at, why it very fast, if it showed itself, would be displaced, whether this would be like so many other pains, through drinking or drugs, etc. Will think that these personalities are only too aware of their pain, and not as those who suppress it, for they live in hiding from themselves and assume an imagination of a good feeling that does not even eliminate the existence of reality. It must be to be lonely without being lonely, that is, the denial of the feeling of loneliness even if one is not physically lonely. Can such a personality be sidelined with people who push others away so as not to acknowledge the feeling, that is, that such a personality makes themselves lonely so as not to become lonely? Can be difficult to see, since other things can play a role in such things, such as the most widespread, responsibilities as in obligations.

Personally, I've always been lonely, both lonely without being lonely, lonely from the feeling of loneliness because being alone, standing outside, not being part of the "unity", maybe? The latter, probably not exactly something I would think is or can be a direct cause of the feeling of loneliness, since I myself am the cause of the feeling, which therefore cannot be completely put under this, even if not belonging to or being understood, probably always will be the cause of other things.

My own loneliness started in childhood and not as a feeling of loneliness or a real perception of being lonely, although it has always been in the back of my mind for no reason to become conscious, but it was more of a start that made me distinctive and later cause to a loneliness that was only reinforced in the face of the outside world, that is, falsity, deception, and neglect, and much else in the direction that then came to the feeling of loneliness again after a few years all alone. And it is also something of a twisted feeling that is only understandable that some people want to push/displace since it is about one's identity and therefore not something that will be easy. To "shift" something so fundamental of the self will actually require it to lie to the person from childhood or during development, in order to maintain a false identity image, and yet I imagine that it is still just below the surface and waiting.

I'm still blank with what makes/gives us this feeling of loneliness if we all really have it, whether this is something that comes first with age or due to certain events in life? Maybe the "experience" of not being single is what makes us aware that we are lonely, which maybe for some is to find oneself in another, but which can also be the personal/mental, which must then have something to do, to be different from the "normal"?

I am lonely as I am because I choose not to change it to the point that I know will not be good for me, and so loneliness is also associated with very few torments. The feeling of loneliness, on the other hand, is a little outside one's own regulations, kind of, because it requires acceptance, the acceptance that we as human are different, and that we must accept each other as we are, within the norms, but whose norms? But it certainly also requires that one accept oneself as who one are, for can one not that, nothing else matters, but it depends a lot on who one are, for with the habit of not being accepted, one can only as a curious person accepts oneself as who one is.

Just some thoughts, but are you lonely or what is the reason you are or is not?

# 12 LIVE

(December 2, 2015)

## We are born and we die, but do we live?

Life is a weird size, a life we are born into and which is not for life but for consumption, a consumption that no one for themselves is willing to put over their lives, even if their lives are controlled by the need, as if no one else existence is possible.

We are all born as an empty shall, act primarily on our own impulses and through this response learned from the outside world. We learn everything we become, until we become who we are, the foundations of our personality are laid down, and everything we then learn is based on this "becoming".

We may learn new things, but the learning process is still based on whom and what each of us is, which affects our emotions and the reaction from and on our emotions. We learn the basic pattern of behavior that once thrives in the majority that our parents have also learned, right or wrong doesn't really matter, because it is still the reality for the individual whether this is the person who learned it or whether it is another person who has learned something else, which only creates condemnation based on what is more right than wrong.

Some personalities do not find acceptance in themselves to be able or willing to acknowledge that, who we are or have become, and for the reason that pleases the feeling best, creates illusions that disclaims themselves or their cares responsibility/guilt whether this is learned or for emotional reasons is of no real importance for life, especially to the life that must dissociate from life due to lack of responsibility for life.

Funny enough, "the one" who has learned most sensibly on the emotional level is a major influence or aided in affirming this kind of denial of reality, in their otherwise good compassion in wanting to protect the one who denies, since reality here is mostly is too cruel to recognize why an illusion is created and kept alive through affirmation of equality and personalities that show understanding through pity, which at societal level bears greater responsibility than the denial, as everything else will be seen only as condemnation and not something human, for is it truly human to lead a person behind the light or to make a person stay in self-deception? Isn't it really one's own sense of emotional need that is covered by disregarding reality through pity to show compassion to others?

Obviously, this topic will never be straightforward and without self-anguish, even for the more emotionally correct, as unheard subjects will never be seen as kindness or as something exhibited by an emotionally correct personality, which can really only give the thought whether the one who shows compassion is actually the most emotionally correct personality, or just the one who lives in an illusion?

How can we really know what is right and wrong on the emotional level? Clearly I know how I feel about a certain subject or at some point, but can I show how I should feel because someone else or most "says" that is how they feel and therefore also the most correct to feel?

It causes many conflicts, and not only in itself, having to live in denial of reality, because if we are not the result of what we have learned as a infant, then we are of genes or other different and therefore of different compositions which will not give the same fact.

If, on the other hand, we are a result of what we have learned, we all have the opportunity to feel the same towards the same, there is really no difference between us, no matter race or gender, but this is not the case for the gender. alone makes a difference than just what we have learned and probably also how we should learn, but still not something that is right or wrong, and not at all for the opposite sex, because here it can mostly only be the case that we suppose how the opposite sex is arranged (cognitive).

If we now consider that we are born as empty shells, created by a mix of unbelievable many templates, which is ultimately a mixture of our two parent's templates, there is the foundation of our building in which is determined our way to perceive and act upon, the physical in which the "trajectories" of our brain are also "built", that is, the way we think and process information, which is the cognitive. Now we just can't talk about the cognitive in that sense, since the board is blank as new born, there are only the most basic (primitive) reactions as part of survival. So we are only the core of ourselves first, which then slowly/quickly turns into a symbiosis with the outside world that begins the creation of the self that teaches.

There are some studies that indicate that children who

have not been brought up by their parents have a tendency to develop some kind of mental disorders, which mental disorders must also create in people who have been brought up inappropriately by their parents, that is "embossing" that which is different to who the person is and therefore also has been something that has been different to the parent or parents who have incurred something for the child, the inheritance is inherited. This inheritance can be both due to something "unconscious" which is due to something that is "denied" or something more proven, which is nevertheless the result of a disorder that is denied by the person who denies/displaces.

Who are we as a single individual? Everyone will say that they know who they are, but are really just who they are willing to believe they are, or is it just now, only myself who believe I am who I think I am and not who I know I am? Where do we set the limit for who we are? Like, if I acknowledge that I am who I am and based on this realization, everything and everyone else is defined from my realization, so if my realization is just an assumption, my whole reality is a built-up illusion!

I know that my life is not based on an illusion and also that I do not belong to the majority responsible for life, so the likelihood that I live in denial of myself is much less than in those responsible who define what there is right and wrong and that everything should be the same for everyone. So from this presentation, I can confirm to myself that my assumptions are mostly of common sense and from this, continue in my thoughts about how strange life is basically arranged.

I have met many, who are only a very, very small part, of all who are, but of those I have met, there are so many who believe they are who they think they are, and also consider their surroundings from this view by themselves. And might as well introduce myself to this I touched on pity, to "add" people's convictions for the sake of peace, because it is really bad to touch something delicate to a person who denies/suppresses, no matter how positive and careful one tries to express such a thing, as it promotes the direct hatred and hostility of the person who hears everything but what is said, they do not want the feelings that arise in them, in such situations, to be their own, which therefore becomes "applied/transmitted" to the person who makes them aware of themselves.

Defense in this world is diverse, and not a single person can really say that they do not contain any kind of defense, for we are all inflicted and influenced throughout life. It is more about being willing to do something about oneself and changing to who one really are. What is probably most surprising to me is that what is closest is actually also the one that has the least interest, that is, one's self and not with the thoughts in the consumption/desire or the need that really only worsens.

Many years ago, when I became aware of all the disorders that are "titles" on in society, I would not accept that people cannot change, found and still find it incredibly difficult to understand that something so close to one is also what people deny the most. Well, then, could it be incredibly appealing to picture myself being something I am not, but does it change my reality? Maybe if I've always been like that, even though I still can't see it changing anything, either about my world or my person, maybe just an imaginary emotional pleasure?

Clearly, change cannot happen without a person being willing to make a difference, to realize and create change in themselves, which only begs the question, what can one actually allow as a person to do to other people? Almost everyone would tell a blind person that if they continue on their path, that they will fall over the edge, is there any difference? Perhaps it is only a matter of love that true love would also have an understanding of the compassion of others? Explains much from a part of this world/society...

Within philosophy, reference is often made to René Descarte's words of the fifteenth century "Cogito, ergo sum - I think, therefor I am." in the context with consciousness, that is, because you think, then you are, but this has nothing to do with consciousness, and therefore you cannot say because you think more thoughts then a person who only thinks one thought, that you then are more conscious than the other, because, as I said, it has nothing to do with consciousness. Therein, only the content of thought can be a sign of the extent of consciousness.

Consciousness is because of our senses, our emotions, which may or may not have been suppressed, and therefore also limit our consciousness, where the denial of reality, of and whether oneself are the greatest sinners, for through the acceptance of who you are, becomes the recognition also of who you were, then who you "are" can no longer be who you "are", when you have acknowledged who you "were", the change lies in recognition.

*"Everything that I have hitherto considered to be the most true and secure, I have learned from the senses. But sometimes I have come to know that the senses have deceived me, and it is wise never to rely completely on it, there just once have fooled us. - Descartes "*

We live and die, yes and some will say: yes we do then and then we come to heaven, hell or be born again, but it doesn't really matter!? We live now and it is the moment that is the most important and which should be what the center of all is. And besides that, one would also assume that if something were to be found after death which is as "enticement" as what is always presented, then something like a form of gain without effort, and therefore the bottom of the bottom and not the top of the top, is not something to be associated with consumption, but something to be "earned" or something to be achieved, that it, through a certain dignity as a human being. Yesterday is what choice for today is the direction of tomorrow, so the direction of life is right now, every single day...

# 13 LUNACY

(January 3, 2015)

## Psychopath/insane

The psychopathic condition has become very widespread in the world today and it is only getting worse and worse, this is due to, among other things, the upbringing or lack thereof, the world increasingly consists of "the self" and only "the self", money and titles, which in itself is the cornerstone of a psychopathic structure, why should it then become smaller?

It has become normal to be a psychopath, and the "normal" has become ill, how can a psychopath living in a notion of being normal see that they have problems?

It is usually easy to figure out a psychopath, especially those who really think they have no problem, because they do not live in fear of being seen, which is why it is so obvious, thus for anyone who is not a psychopath themselves!

You can see it in a different way. Psychiatry makes a diagnosis according to a system which states certain "concepts" that must be "fulfilled" in order for a term to be applied to a person. A scale of, for example, 10 things that a person should "contain" can therefore provide an indicator of the degree of dysfunctional personality there is defined.

Without getting into these "indications", you can try to interpret this.

From this scale, which contains the number 1 to 10, we can put a degree on a personality, without interpreting whether the number 10 is higher than the number 1, assuming that if a person has the content in under the number 10, and another a person has the contents of the number 1, so that it cannot be said directly that the person with the number 10 is a bigger psychopath than the person with the number 1 on them, but on the other hand if one person has only one number and another has two numbers, then the person with the two numbers is a greater degree of psychopath than the person with only one number. However, it can be debated whether the "term" as a single number contains has a greater impact on the human psyche and therefore weighs more important in topics such as ethics/morals and therefore can make the content under a single number be said to be so important to the human Psyche that this alone can be designated a psychopathic condition!

Before the point of what I have mentioned here, it should be added that the content of this schema according to which a personality is described as dysfunctional personality is chained the same and fits into the structure that just touch a psychopathic personality, of which understanding is a large part of this. Not being able to see anything other than what creates their actions, that is, it also affects understanding or lack of understanding, it is the cognitive, the way the brain functions, the way it processes information that a psychopath will always circulate around the self, that is no action, no thought expressed, without affecting the psychopath's own self. Such a person will or can never do anything without ultimately promoting the self!

But the point as mentioned with the scale is (little black and white interpretation), how many numbers should a person be assigned so that the personality cannot see that another personality with larger numbers assigned is not a psychopath? Meaning, if the person include 5 terms from this scale, the person would then look at a person with 6 numbers assigned as a psychopath or maybe 10 more numbers, or will the personality have so much of a basic case that this person will be seen as more normal or just one that the other personality would seek towards? The personalities have the same view since the personalities both possess things from such a scale, so when is the morality so distant that nothing abnormal is seen about it? How far down in numbers should we be before a personality start seeing another personality with multiple numbers assigned, as being a sick personality?

Personally, I do everything in my power, not to have anything to do with some of these concepts, maybe that's why I often see more psychopathic tendencies than others are willing, because there are basic things to a greater understanding of a person's personality where it can be safely said that if a person exhibits a "thing" that they then possess psychopathic personality!

You can find many different formulations of the psychopathic state, and this has not been made better by the media's tendency to also give their interpretation of this type of personality, without having any major thoughts on what they actually portray to people (or do they), for it is not so much what is said, it is more what you are willing to believe or how your understanding of words and concepts is. You also have to think that a psychopath distorts things, they turn things to their own advantage, just to cover up who they are, and they also seek power, so if in the beginning of time there was a sincere description of a psychopathic personality, then you can be assured that an incredible number of attempts have been made to distort this view in order to make you believe differently. Wouldn't it be best for the "self-conscious psychopath" to live a normal life without others seeing it as abnormal? The use of the word "self-conscious" is because the vast majority of psychopaths are self-conscious about their personality, which is why they do exactly what they can to hide themselves, an unconscious psychopath, as mentioned, lives in a notion that there is nothing wrong with it. is normal to be so. Here we can actually talk more about the schizophrenic area, without being schizophrenic, but lack of insight into illnesses and delusions etc.

The psychopath is found in the amount of the majority, for is it not in the social that the psychopath thrives?

# ABOUT THE AUTHOR

Yes, who am I? Isn't that the question for all of us, who are we! For am I not who I am because you are who you are? Or am I just who I am, based on who you think you are, whereby I am nothing but what you think you are. So the question is probably more, who are you? Now you know a little of whom I am.

If, on the other hand, you ask me, what are you: I am nothing but what I am, that is who I am, nothing.

www.ingramcontent.com/pod-product-compliance
Lightning Source LLC
Chambersburg PA
CBHW070755250726
48662CB00004B/1825